A FLASH OF LIFE

LANI KAUTEN

Cover image by Russ Kauten

A Flash of Life
Copyright © 2022 by Lani Kauten

Library of Congress Control Number:	2022907585
ISBN-13: Paperback:	978-1-64749-708-8
ePub:	978-1-64749-709-5

All rights reserved. No part of this publication may be reproduced, distributed, or transmitted in any form or by any means, including photocopying, recording, or other electronic or mechanical methods, without the prior written permission of the publisher or author, except in the case of brief quotations embodied in critical reviews and certain other noncommercial uses permitted by copyright law.

Although every precaution has been taken to verify the accuracy of the information contained herein, the author and publisher assume no responsibility for any errors or omissions. No liability is assumed for damages that may result from the use of information contained within.

Printed in the United States of America

GoToPublish LLC
1-888-337-1724
www.gotopublish.com
info@gotopublish.com

Here's what's been said and written about
Lani Kauten's
"A Flash of Life"

In Lani Kauten's twenty-five page *Flash of Life* (2018), for no known reason, Lani starts having terrorizing dreams that involve her brother. He has always been her soulmate, confidante, dependably there to comfort her whenever she is worried. She has no idea why dreams filled with violence, peopled with threatening faces she can't decipher as they wiz by in a blur, would involve him. Every night, after who knows how long, they reach a climax that awakens her, sweating and shaking, and refusing to go back to sleep for fear they return.

"When I try to reach out to find you, lights from passing windows much like those of an airplane appear."

She tries reaching him but fails at every turn. In fact, he seems to have disappeared. When the dreams take a dramatic turn to night terrors like she's never before had, and always, in the 3 a.m. hour, she becomes desperate to find her brother. Partly, this is because she's frightened something has happened to him, and another part because she hopes finding him will end the night terrors.

"I've gone by your house a dozen times hoping that if I saw you, somehow it would put an end to these night terrors. But instead I'm met with endless loops of unanswered doorbell rings, and my calls forwarded to your answering machine."

But that is only part of the story. As Lani shares her desperate search, she explores with us the close relationship the two siblings had, one she always thought would last forever:

"...The house where we forged that bond between brother and sister that I thought we'd have into our old age. ... Where I waited for you every day to come home from school. "Look what I learned today,

Johnny." I would say. "I learned how to do a cartwheel. See." You were always so attentive."

Where did it go so wrong that these precious memories are now fodder for her deadly treacherous dreams?

This story called to me because I feel this same way about a brother I thought was my soulmate. His 'disappearance' is not physical but no less upsetting. I have no doubt Lani's emotional words and gripping story will resonate with lots of people like me.

- Jacqui Murray

Well written, poignant story. Had me in tears.

I was caught by the first words and pulled into the story. It made me recall all the times I shared with my own big brother, and reminded me to give him a call and tell him I love him.

The author captures the nostalgia of growing up with a loved sibling, and the reality of how we just don't talk as much as we used to.

Five stars is the most I could give, but for the emotional tugs, I would have given it ten if I could.

- CJ

Very well if you are Lani Kauten. I found my heart to be beating faster during the dreaming parts of the book. Felt like I was waiting for something to drop. Like when you're in trouble. When you know something horrible is going to happen. But then that all stops, when you read those moments of this sister and brother. I never had a sibling growing up. But these memories, these emotions and thoughts, were everything I thought it would be like. What I wished for. I just want to thank you for sharing what it's like to have that kind of love of a sibling. And mostly for a sibling. This will stay with me. This feeling you gave me. So thank you!

- **Saird**

A FLASH OF LIFE

Dreams are just dreams they say, but my nightmares weren't just dreams.

ONE

John, since my waking nightmares started about you, they've only intensified, rather than diminish over these last several nights, and always start in a place where you're obscured by the shadows thick in the air. When I try to reach out to find you, lights from passing windows much like those of an airplane appear. The savagery of fear grabs hold of me, and I hold back my reach, squeeze my eyes shut too horrified to look at the unfamiliar faces, but I do, every single time and it's at that moment I'm pulled through a vacuum of air sucking the life out of my lungs. I wake gasping for air, drenched in my sweat and sit straight up in bed. I throw back my covers and stare into the darkness of my bedroom, daring to look at the alarm clock. It's never exactly the same time but always during the three o'clock hour. Dread inevitably follows because I can't save you.

Tonight I forced myself to stay awake. Unlike the previous nights, the passing windows flashed by at unnerving speeds. Then stopped, intentionally, right before me for just a fraction of time to show me the faces of people staring back. I reached out to trace the face directly in front of me in hopes of remembering him once I've awakened. But it never fails, his image always blurs together with the rest.

TWO

I've gone by your house a dozen times hoping that if I saw you, somehow it would put an end to these night terrors. But instead I'm met with endless loops of unanswered doorbell rings, and my calls forwarded to your answering machine. You've always been kind of a loner, I get that. But this, this is something well out of your character. Before, when I'd call, you'd respond within a couple days. Now, zilch!

I've racked my brain trying to figure out what's changed so dramatically in your life to cause such behavior. Though, if I'm going to be honest with myself, your connection with me and the family fell away deliberately, slowly, piece by piece sometime ago. Maybe these dreams are making me confront why that might be, and I haven't the slightest idea how to fix this, John. I'm hoping writing this letter will help pull you out of whatever funk you're in, and make me feel better about this horrific roller coaster ride about you because it's driving me to the fringe of insanity.

You survived the '60s and helped pull me through the '70s. We shared everything about anything. Remember.

I'll always be your bratty little sister, I know that. But I want it all back. Our quirky conversations, the laughter, our teasing-well, your teasing anyway. God, I hope it's not too late.

Gehringer Street, my first memories of you, teaching me how to tie my shoes just before I started kindergarten. The house where we forged that bond between brother and sister that I thought we'd have into our old age. Where I waited for you every day to come home from school. "Look what I learned today, Johnny." I would say. "I learned how to do a cartwheel. See." You were always so attentive.

Remember how Mom's creative mind was always spinning, which kept us and the neighborhood kids happily entertained. Especially the day when she recruited the whole lot of us-even our cousins who lived around the corner-to help convert our spare bedroom into a makeshift grocery store. We helped her build shelving with those cement blocks almost as big as I was and scraps of wood we collected from around the neighborhood. It took awhile, but Mom saved every empty egg carton and detergent soap box and canned goods to display until it looked just like a real grocery store. She even stuffed newspaper into the empty bread loaf bags to make it look like real bread. She searched high and low for a cash register and found that old-green antique with the drawer that dinged when it opened. She went as far as to put coins in the drawer just for us to learn how to make change. Everyone loved taking turns on the cash register. I knew the store was more for me and my friends, than you, being six years older and all. But you played right along and still pretended with me.

I have this foggy memory where I'm sitting on our salt and pepper colored rug in the living room, and you called me over to look out the living room window. I saw Dad helping Mom out of the car, and she was holding something wrapped in a pink blanket and I thought it was a doll for me! Being only five at the time, I never paid much mind to Mom being pregnant. But I was so excited to learn that that doll was a real baby. Our sister Lehua. Do you remember this?

You and I spent all of our time getting acquainted with her and found out very fast that she cried . . . a lot! And we quickly realized we'd much rather be outside playing with our friends.

She couldn't have been a day over a year, when we pleaded with Mom to let us take her to the junior high school right behind our house, to push her around in the stroller.

"She's too small for you two to handle," Mom pointed out. But we persisted. Even pleaded at the top of our lungs, till we finally convinced her otherwise.

We pushed Lehua in her stroller up and down those hallways. Remember the one that sloped? The one we didn't know was in full view of our house. We pushed her down that hallway over and over again just to hear her contagious laugh when her stroller hit the lockers. She got such a kick out of it, and our bellies ached from all the laughing. However, we were so busy entertaining each other that we never noticed Mom peering over the fence watching in pure horror.

Mom sure gave us a piece of her mind when she met up with us walking down the sidewalk, shaking her finger towards us.

"What were you two thinking?" yelling at the top of her lungs. "You could've hurt your baby sister!" Grabbing the stroller away from us, she shouted, "Get in the house."

Yet, you took all the blame telling her, "It was all my idea, Ma."

We were scared to death over the trouble we knew we were in. Nonetheless, we still giggled with each other on our way into the house over the fun we had. Life of being a kid, yeah. I can still hear the echoes of our laughter racing Lehua up and down those halls.

Johnny! Pleeease! For me! Dig deep down into the soul of the man I know you are and bring back that boy. The boy that would've stopped at nothing to protect me.

THREE

Remember the day Dad came home after work and told us we were getting a swimming pool and how excited we were? Until I found out in order to build the pool my favorite tree (the Weeping Willow that I climbed on every day) had to come out. I cried and hugged the tree as tightly as I could, hoping hugging it would save it. But you stood there under the tree with me and helped me understand why it had to come out. I cried nonetheless.

Experts say you never remember all your dreams you've had the night before you awake, but you can call to mind some of them explicitly.

The only part of my dream that I couldn't recall were the faces in the windows, because they always blurred together the moment I awoke. But tonight, when the windows stopped moving for that fleeting moment, the blank inscrutable face staring back at me was yours, John. I was chilled to the bone, and my heart pounded so hard I could hear it between my ears. Distraught, I tried to stay awake, but my body finally succumbed from pure exhaustion only to be terror-stricken out of sleep again by the flash of your face. My brain waves only seem to know one path now to take me down while sleeping. Where the speeding windows stop for that instant.

I reach over to check the time . . . huh, 3:30 A.M. I rub my eyes and lie there for a couple of minutes wondering why this particular time of night has fused together with my dreams about you, but got nothing, Zip! I sit up and patted my sweaty face. My nightgown feels damp against my skin as I make my way down the stairs. I just couldn't take another awakening tonight, so here I sit at my kitchen table, and aimlessly rummage through Halloween decorations I've yet to put away. Only one thought went round and round in my mind, until the first sign of light. Three-thirty. Frustrated, I pocket that thought and went back upstairs to dress for work.

FOUR

Our worst day, when Mom and Dad told us we were moving across town turned out to be the best day after they took us to see the house.

"It's brand new!" you hollered out with excitement while we ran from room to room, Lehua tagging behind. Her two-year old legs could hardly keep up.

"This one's mine," I said, flopping onto the floor and immediately feeling the heat generating up from the pipes underneath it. You followed suit.

"This is outta sight!" we both yelled, and looked over to each other and laughed. I've never seen so many windows, especially windows that went from floor to ceiling. (A signature design of an Eichler home.)

We were anxious to start our new schools, and being there was only a couple months left until summer break made it worse. I now know even though you hid it well, it was harder on you being in eighth grade meeting new friends than me being in second grade.

The house on Lancashire was much bigger than the one on Gehringer Street, and it felt like a mansion to us. Dad already had plans to build us an even bigger pool to accommodate the slide we were getting. It got underway right away, and every day after school there was something new. Until it had finally taken on the shape it was going to be—kidney.

Before we knew it, the night came when the fire department hooked up their hose to the hydrant and let the water flow into our brand new pool. The sight of the fire truck filled the neighborhood with excitement and thrilled some of the neighbors enough to come into the backyard and watch the spectacle. What fun we had whooshing down the slide into the heated blue water.

We swam every day during the summer with our friends, but nighttime was the best, especially when we turned off the pool light and all the lights in the house to make it seem even spookier. Mom and Dad were always cool about letting us do things like that. Remember.

I was always hanging about when your friends came over. Sometimes you were alright with it, but other times you weren't. You never knew this, but my first crush was on one of your friends: Jeff, I think his name was.

Everyone loved our backyard with the tropical theme, palm trees included. They said it reminded them of Hawai'i. Of course it didn't hurt that Mom was from there. Some of the neighbors thought her plants would never last, that the Northern California winters were too cold, despite the fact that Ma had a way with gardening. She was sure they would all survive, which they did.

Remember your wedding reception in the backyard? I do! The hottest day of the summer of '71: the same month I turned fourteen. Remember how excited everyone was seeing the big furniture delivery truck arrive? They all gathered around outside to see Grandpa's dining set wedding gift. The photographer took pictures of Connie and you sitting on the chairs holding hands across the table after it was placed in Mom and Dad's living room, and another, of you two kissing while still holding hands. Two of my favorite shots of Connie and you. It was crazy fun watching some of the guests jump in the swimming pool after they had a few drinks. They couldn't help themselves; it was too inviting. I even sneaked a beer to drink that day!

We were beside ourselves with excitement when Mom and Dad told us we'd be spending the Christmas holidays in Hawai'i. We were finally going to see the island of Oahu where Mom was from, and excited to meet her family for the first time.

We learned how to surf and speak Pidgin. Till today, Hawai'i was the most exciting place for me to celebrate New Year's. Remember our uncle and aunties house? All that day everyone kept busy weaving makeshift lines back and forth and up and down their hilly streets, to hang firecrackers and then lit them precisely at midnight. It all made sense then, as to why everyone spent all day stringing lines. The valley was a beautiful display of sparkly-lights, and what a thrill it was to see.

I never knew until I was older that the big storm that hit while we were staying with Grandpa and Grandma in Wahiawa during Christmas, was a hurricane. At the time I thought it was just a storm that hovered right above Grandpa's house. The wind and rain were so strong, like nothing I'd ever heard before, and it got louder and louder—so loud the humming noise from the wind hurt my ears. The windows shook, and the rain hit them so hard it sounded like beating drums, yet they held strong. I always thought Grandpa was mad telling us in his firm heavy accented voice. "We all hunker down here together and be still." Instead, it was because he was worried and wanted us all to be safe.

The next morning when we went outside it was scary to see all the standing water everywhere and the damage to all the other homes.

"Why does our home look like this and those homes," I pointed, "over there look like something ate them?"

Dad tried to explain why some homes were untouched by the storm without alarming me. Nevertheless, it was still a mystery to me at the time. You gave me comfort that everything was okay by holding my hand.

For some reason we had to go into town. One vision still sticks with me today; a woman ankle deep in mud digging out her pots and pans in the valley below the road we took into town.

FIVE

John, Dad just called me, alarmed and confused about a message he and Mom found on their answering machine after returning home from running errands. When I arrived at the house and listened to the message, I too, was confused. The woman's voice was fuzzy sounding. Incoherent. It took several times replaying the message before I could make heads or tails of the phone number to call back.

With a gasp, I repeated word for word to Mom and Dad as the person on the other end of the phone relayed, that you had been brought into their hospital after being involved in an automobile accident and that you had suffered trauma to the head, though, had since checked yourself out against the doctors' advice.

"What?"

The nurse repeated the information one more time. I hung up in disbelief and looked over at Dad standing near Mom sitting on the couch, looking exactly how I felt. Bewildered.

"Who does that?" I said shaking my head wondering where you were.

Then you walked through the front door.

Flabbergasted, I ran up to hug you, but instantly felt ashamed that it took this long to put together the pieces. So I blurted out, "We just found out what happened." Hoping it would make everything okay as to why we weren't there for you! That I wasn't there for you.

Still shaken, we sat down to hear what you had to say about the accident. I fixated on your face while you told your story. *There was so much I wanted to tell you. So much I needed to ask.* Instead, regretfully, I just listened and watched your every move. You continued on.

"The report stated I was unconscious the whole time while the Fire Department used the Jaws of Life to pry me out of my car. The witnesses reported that it was a huge utility truck that ran over the back-half part of my car. You then gestured with your hand as to how it propelled your car into oncoming traffic. The last thing I remembered is looking under my dashboard from the floorboard. The highway was a tangled mess of metal."

I had you in my grasp, and yet all I could muster in the end was, "Why'd you check yourself out?"

You looked me square in the eye. "Because I feel fine. Dad, can you give me a ride home?"

"That's it!" Mom said. She looked over to Dad with that all too familiar look in her eyes, that we've learned over time meant that she's yelling at him to do something, without actually yelling.

But you stood up and Dad walked with you out the door. My brother, the man of few words.

I was frustrated over your resoluteness to put this whole experience behind you, and disappointed at myself in letting the opportunity go by without expressing my concerns over the nightmares I've been having about you.

The next night though the dreams came back vividly different. There were no lights from windows speeding by this time. Instead, there was a flash of light that flooded the deepest, darkest crevices around me that had kept you obscured. I reached out and touched your face and traced your freckles, as subtle as they were. A trait you always hated, but I needed to know that face, those freckles were yours. In my mind's eye. Your mouth moved but no sound came out, and I found myself once again in the obscurity of darkness. I yelled for you as loud as I could over and over . . . *Johnny, Johnny!* But I couldn't find you nor feel your presence this time. I awoke in a lurch, actually crying your name out loud which awakened Russ. I usually never disturbed him when I woke out of these dreams, I always filled him in later, so he was shaken to his core to see 3:15 A.M. flashing back at him from the bedside clock. It all finally sank in.

"Maybe there's something to this three o'clock hour after all," he said, as he comforted me in the security of his arms. The tears took longer to get under control. The next day I drove by your house on my way home from work to check and see how you were feeling. I knocked, but you didn't answer. I looked in your living room window. Your coffee table was cluttered with leftover take out, some empty glasses, indicating you hadn't eaten alone. I didn't see you anywhere, so I left.

"John!" I yelled into my phone. "I need to talk to you real bad. Pleeease call me back."

Then hung up. *You need to know about my dreams,* I shouted inside my head. I didn't know why, but I flashed back to the clutter on your table of *empty take-out boxes and drinking glasses, and an ashtray full of cigarette butts, and cigarette ash lying around it.* What else was there I didn't want to see, and am I even ready to hear anything other than I'm tired . . . been working too hard, the accident was harder on me than I thought.

While driving home on my lunch hour I passed you on the freeway. Remember. I was extremely elated to see you, even if it was on the

A FLASH OF LIFE

freeway. I motioned for you to follow me home for lunch. You tapped at your wrist, indicating to me that you didn't have time. Disappointed, I exited the freeway and watched your car move past me.

SIX

The next day, Saturday November 7, 1992 (forever imprinted in my brain,) the phone rang, and Russ answered it. Covering the mouth piece, he whispered to me, "It's your dad. He sounds funny," as he handed the phone to me.

"Hey, Dad, what's up?"

"It's your brother."

My heart skipped, but confounded by your aloofness. I put up a tough side and said, "What is it now?"

"We need to go down and identify him at Memorial Hospital."

My eye-glasses flew off my face as I hung up the phone. I heard this guttural scream . . . "My brother's dead!" Then realized those words were coming up from out of my throat. It was surreal. I cupped my face into my hands, and tears were already streaming down. It was all simultaneous—my voice yelling. The million jumbled memories of you vividly racing through my head, all in a flash: In '75, my first day on the job site (in my blue jeans, work boots and a hard hat) working for Dad. You giving me thirty second instructions on how to operate a cement

Clary and walking away with that confident smile you always had on your face, saying, "Good luck!" Floating on top of that huge-orange life jacket making my way around the pool coping at the Gehringer house, and you swimming next to me. You in your black and white converse shoes sitting cross-legged next to me teaching me how to tie my shoes. Laughing and swimming with Connie and her sisters and brother, even though it had been years since your divorce.

I barely remember hanging up the phone, rushing to my bedroom, and putting on my running shoes. As I ran by the telephone in our kitchen, I thought ... Lehua doesn't know yet. I don't even remember pushing the numbers, nor hearing the phone ring on the other end, when a voice said:

"Hello."

"Lehua"... I barely gurgled through convulsing sobs. "No, it's George."

The next voice I heard was our baby sister.

"Oh Lehua" ... more sobs heave up my throat ... "John—Johnny passed away." For a moment on the other end, the phone line was so silent, it was deafening. I was shaking all over, and all I wanted to do was run. Russ grabbed the phone and I heard him say what hospital it was just as I flew out the front door and raced to Mom and Dad's house. It was crazy because they lived five miles away, yet I didn't care. All I wanted was to get to them as fast as I could. And running seemed logical. Russ and Jessi (our daughter,) caught up to me in the car, as I was running up the hill around the corner from our house.

As soon as I entered the house I could see Mom and Dad moving about in the kitchen, clearly showing signs of shock. Through utter silence, I helped them gather some of their personal effects and pretty much poured them into our car. I don't remember much of the ride over to the hospital. Just the quite.

At the hospital when the doctor greeted us, he explained the situation. I think I heard every other word. He then asked if we'd like to go in now and see you. Those words made it undeniable. None of us moved. We just stared at one another. Pure fear glued my feet to the floor. I looked over to Mom and clearly saw that she was in no condition to make that journey first. So we both sat in the chairs directly behind us, and Jessi sat next to me. Out of the corner of my eye I saw your girlfriend Renee walking towards us, all red-faced from tears and a runny nose. She sat on the other side of Mom. I held Mom's hands, and watched Dad as the doctor walked Dad and Russ down the short hallway to the curtain.

The hands on the clock on the wall across from us, tick-tocked and everyone around continued about, though time literally stopped for me and sounds muffled. I looked over at Mom, fixated at the curtain down the hall, completely traumatized, with watery eyes. Her hands tightly clutched around mine.

When I looked down the hall to see what she was so fixated on I saw a sliver of your face through the drawn curtain. My throat tightened making it hard to swallow, and I panicked. Goosebumps ran amok all over my body, and I sat there and stared through that sliver-opening, and shouted inside my head. *John, please get up.*

"Move!" Not realizing I muttered that word.

Mom then locked arms with me like trying to tell me *it's okay, you're speaking for me, too.*

I tried to be quiet but the words kept falling out of my mouth. "Please John, just sit up and smile that smile of yours." *You have two beautiful daughters to watch grow up,* I thought, and I didn't even want to have to make that call to Nicole and Samantha. "Please just open your eyes. Look at me, say something, anything." I pleaded as I blotted my wet face with an already soaked tissue. But you never did.

Russ told me that Dad looked upon his only son with a tube down his throat, a needle in his neck, and more in both of his arms and uttered, "Oh my little boy," while rubbing your face with the backside of his hand.

He said, "The doctor asked, is this your son?" "Yes . . . this is my Johnny boy."

"Your dad then, bent down, kissed your brother's cheek and whispered, 'I love you.' He looked at me with wet eyes, then looked back at the doctor and said in the softest voice, 'He just turned forty-one. Did you know that?' He patted John's head, then turned and left the room."

Choked up and wiping his tears away, it took a moment for Russ to collect himself enough to say, "That was the hardest thing I've ever done, but I'm glad I was there for your father during a very private moment with his son."

It took every bit of strength I had to pull myself out of my seat, and it had to be even harder on Mom. Arm in arm we made our way down what felt like the longest walk toward the drawn curtain. I was surprised when we stepped through the curtain to find a nurse standing in the corner of the room waiting very quietly, exhibiting such compassion for us. Mom nearly collapsed to the floor when she saw you. Russ warned me, but it was still shocking to see everything they used to try and save your life, still impaled in your body. I asked the nurse why, and she told me that only the Coroner can remove them. I kissed your freckled cheek and glanced one more time upon your handsome face, then leaned in close to your ear and ever so quietly through my tears promised you: "I will always be here for your girls." I was very thankful the nurse was there to help console Mom. She gave you one last hug and squeezed your hand and walked out. I took one last look at you, whispered, "Goodbye Johnny," and followed Mom.

I think I know what three thirty meant. The last thing that Renee said to me at your funeral stopped me cold. That you had been unable to sleep those last several nights, because of a bad migraine, and that you found playing games on the TV helped you forget about the pain. She also added that that night you played the games during 3:00 A.M. before coming back to bed. It wasn't till later when I put my arm around your brother that I realized he wasn't breathing. We both hugged each other, and sobbed.

It was confirmed by the Coroner that you met your fate with a brain aneurysm, most likely caused from the trauma your head took from the car accident.

A flash of your life, brother, until we meet again.

ABOUT THE AUTHOR

Lani Kauten grew up in Concord when it was a small town in Northern California, around a tight-knit family, with an open-door policy to family and friends. This later encouraged the foundation to write. Kauten is also a long-standing member of *Write On* and *California Writers Circle* of Orange County. She worked as an Administrative Assistant for almost thirty years, most of which were in the oil industry.

She launched her first short story, *Breaking Summer*, back in 2014. *Knightfall: Midnight at the Montclaire*, an anthology which is a product of the collaborative efforts of the author and California Writers Circle, is also available on Amazon. She is currently wrapping up her latest book, *The Briefcase*, and is in the process of working on another title, called *The Umbrella Jade*.

She now resides with her family in Orange County, California.

www.ingramcontent.com/pod-product-compliance
Lightning Source LLC
LaVergne TN
LVHW041553060526
838200LV00037B/1278